The Question & Answer Book

OUR AMAZING OCEAN

OUR AMAZING OCEAN

By David Adler
Illustrated by Joseph Veno

Troll Associates

Library of Congress Cataloging in Publication Data

Adler, David A.
  Our amazing ocean.

  (The Question and answer book)
  Summary: Questions and answers provide basic informa-
tion about the ocean, including wave formation, currents,
depth, salinity, marine biology, and its utilization for
humankind.
    1. Ocean—Juvenile literature. [1. Ocean. 2. Ques-
tions and answers] I. Veno, Joseph, ill. II. Title.
III. Series.
GC21.5.A33 1983   551.46   82-17373
ISBN 0-89375-882-5
ISBN 0-89375-883-3 (pbk.)

Printed in the United States of America
10   9   8   7   6   5   4   3   2   1

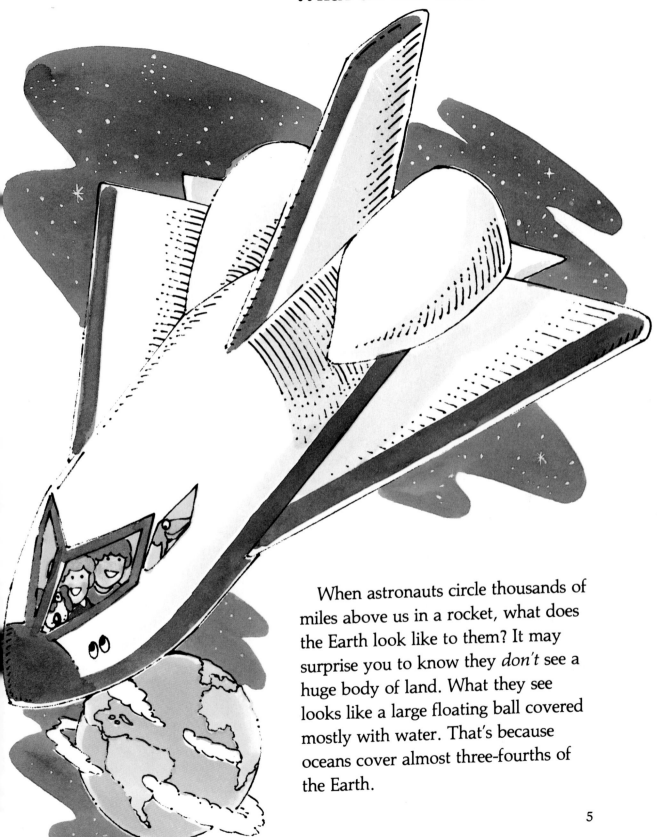

When astronauts circle thousands of miles above us in a rocket, what does the Earth look like to them? It may surprise you to know they *don't* see a huge body of land. What they see looks like a large floating ball covered mostly with water. That's because oceans cover almost three-fourths of the Earth.

Look at the globe, and you'll see what the astronauts see. Most of the globe is colored blue. The blue areas show where water is found.

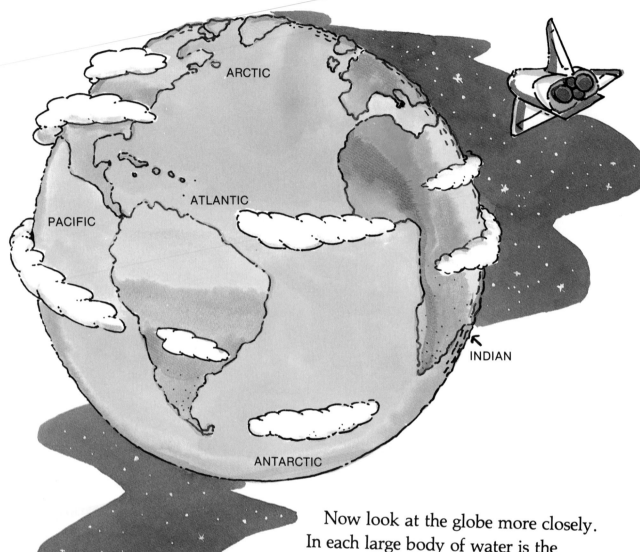

Now look at the globe more closely. In each large body of water is the name of an ocean. The names are Pacific, Atlantic, Indian, Arctic, and Antarctic. Many people say these are the names of five different oceans. But some scientists disagree. They believe these are not five oceans but different parts of one huge ocean.

What do you think?

Place your finger on one of the oceans on a globe. Which ocean is it? Can you move your finger to another ocean without touching land? If you're careful, you'll be able to trace a route through all five oceans and never touch land. That's because all the oceans are connected and form one huge body of water. This is called the world ocean. The largest areas of land, which we call *continents*, are very much like huge islands in this vast ocean.

Water can flow freely from one part of the ocean to another part. Suppose you went to a beach along the east coast of the United States and filled a cup with water from the Atlantic Ocean. The water in your cup may have traveled thousands and thousands of miles. That cupful of water may have once been in the Pacific Ocean. It may have touched the shores of California, New Zealand, or Japan. Or it may have once been in the Indian Ocean—perhaps off the coast of Australia, Java, or Madagascar. Some of the water in that cup might even have melted from an iceberg floating in the Arctic Ocean near the North Pole.

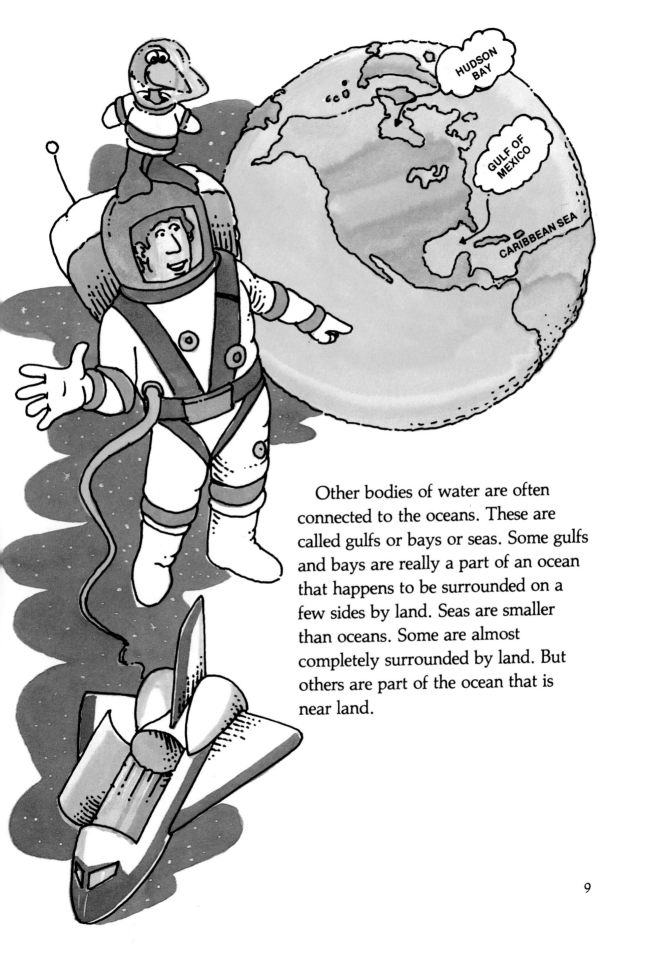

Other bodies of water are often connected to the oceans. These are called gulfs or bays or seas. Some gulfs and bays are really a part of an ocean that happens to be surrounded on a few sides by land. Seas are smaller than oceans. Some are almost completely surrounded by land. But others are part of the ocean that is near land.

What makes the waves?

If you walk along the beach you can learn a lot about the ocean. You will see that the water does not stay still. Waves of water keep washing up on shore. The waves are caused by the wind. In a storm, when the winds are very powerful, ocean waves can become dangerous. Ocean waves in a storm can ruin a beach, tear apart boats, and seriously damage nearby homes.

If you stand in one place near the edge of the water for a while, you will notice another way the water moves. For part of the day, the water moves closer to where you're standing. Then, for the rest of the day, the water moves further away. That movement is called the *tide*. The water will be closest to you at high tide. At low tide it will be furthest away.

In some places, the difference
between high tide and low tide is only
a few inches, or several centimeters. In
other places, like the Bay of Fundy in
Canada, the difference is much greater.
In the Bay of Fundy, a boat could be
resting on dry land at low tide. Later
the same day, at high tide, the boat
could be floating in water as deep as
fifty feet, or fifteen meters.

What causes the tides?

Tides are caused mostly by the moon's *gravity.* The moon's gravity pulls on the Earth, and this gravity also pulls on the water directly below the moon. This makes the ocean bulge out toward the moon. Then it is high tide. As the Earth rotates, different parts of the world face the moon, so the tides are always changing. The sun also pulls on the water. But the sun is much further away than the moon, and its pull is not as great.

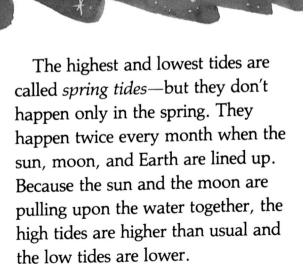

The highest and lowest tides are called *spring tides*—but they don't happen only in the spring. They happen twice every month when the sun, moon, and Earth are lined up. Because the sun and the moon are pulling upon the water together, the high tides are higher than usual and the low tides are lower.

13

The waters of the ocean also move in another way. Powerful streams, called currents, move through the ocean.

Some ocean currents are very large and powerful.

In the Atlantic Ocean, powerful currents form the Gulf Stream. It flows from Florida all the way to Europe.

The Gulf Stream was discovered by Benjamin Franklin. He wondered why it always took less time for American sailors to travel from the colonies to Europe than to sail back home again. He discovered that they were sailing against the powerful Gulf Stream current on the way home. So he told the sailors they would save time by following a much longer route that would let them avoid the Gulf Stream. He was right.

Is there life in the ocean?

In the Gulf Stream, as in much of the world ocean, there are many forms of life. And life in the ocean is very different from life on the land. If you ever walked along a beach, you probably saw long, slimy strands of seaweed washed up on shore. Seaweed is a plant that grows in the ocean.

Seaweed, or algae as it is sometimes called, can be very tiny. It can also grow longer than 300 feet. That's more than a hundred meters! Long ago, sailors were afraid of long strands of seaweed. They thought the seaweed could wrap itself around their boats and keep the boats from moving.

15

Today, we know that seaweed is a valuable resource. It is used in making medicine, fertilizer, and paper. Some people even eat seaweed. It is rich in vitamins and minerals.

Of course, seaweed is not the only form of life in the ocean. The ocean is filled with all kinds of plants and animals. They make up three groups of ocean dwellers: benthos, plankton, and nekton.

Benthos

The *benthos* are the plants and animals that live on the ocean floor. Seaweed is one kind of benthos. But there are many others. Some, like snails, worms, crabs, and lobsters, can move around to find food. Others, like oysters, sponges, and corals, do not move. They must wait for their food to come to them. They eat members of the second group of ocean dwellers— the plankton.

17

Plankton

The *plankton* are plants and animals that drift about in the ocean. Jellyfish are one kind of plankton. But most plankton are too small to be seen— except under a microscope.

Nekton

The *nekton* is the third group of ocean dwellers. It includes animals that swim about in the water. There are octopuses and squids. There are fish and seals. And there are the largest of all the ocean dwellers—the whales.

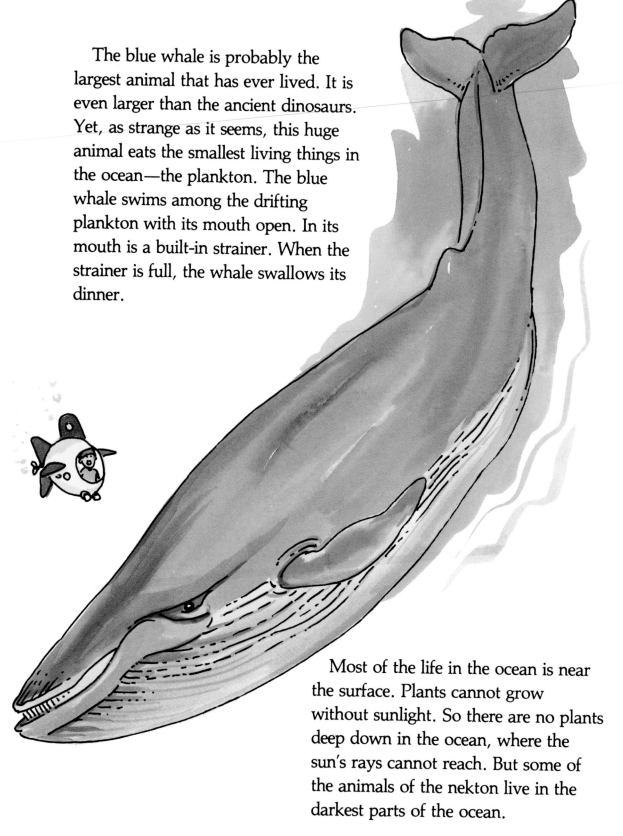

The blue whale is probably the largest animal that has ever lived. It is even larger than the ancient dinosaurs. Yet, as strange as it seems, this huge animal eats the smallest living things in the ocean—the plankton. The blue whale swims among the drifting plankton with its mouth open. In its mouth is a built-in strainer. When the strainer is full, the whale swallows its dinner.

Most of the life in the ocean is near the surface. Plants cannot grow without sunlight. So there are no plants deep down in the ocean, where the sun's rays cannot reach. But some of the animals of the nekton live in the darkest parts of the ocean.

If you ever went swimming in the ocean and swallowed some water, you probably realized at once that ocean water is salty.

How much salt is there in the ocean?

If the ocean dried up and only the salt remained, there would be enough to give millions of boxes of salt to each person living in the United States.

Thousands of years ago, people did take salt from the ocean. In some places they still do. They gather ocean water in ponds. The hot sun evaporates the water, but the salt remains. Then the salt is raked into piles, collected, and cleaned.

How did all that salt get into the ocean?

Scientists believe rain and rivers washed the salt from the land and carried it into the ocean.

Rain and rivers carry other minerals into the ocean, too. In fact, the ocean contains every mineral found on land—including gold. There are enough tiny specks of gold mixed in ocean water to make many people very rich. But it would be very expensive to separate the gold from the water.

In some places, blackish-brown lumps, called *nodules*, lie on the ocean floor. These nodules are made mostly of manganese, a mineral used in making steel.

A machine has been invented to collect the nodules. It's like a huge vacuum cleaner. It sucks the nodules up through a long pipe. Right now there's enough manganese on land. But if land supplies ever run out, there's plenty on the ocean floor, just waiting to be used.

What lies beneath the ocean floor?

Scientists are trying to learn what lies buried beneath the ocean floor. They have already found gold, diamonds, and oil.

It's not easy for scientists to study the ocean floor. In some places it's under thousands of feet of water. It's also not flat. The ocean floor has mountains and valleys and large holes just the way dry land does.

Near most large areas of land, the floor of the ocean is not very deep. It is flat and slopes gently downward. This part of the ocean floor is called the *continental shelf*. Many people consider continental shelves as a part of the land that just happens to be under water.

CONTINENTAL SHELF

CONTINENTAL SLOPE

How deep is the ocean?

As the continental shelf stretches farther from dry land, the water gets gradually deeper. Then the shelf ends and the *continental slope* begins. Here the ocean floor slopes downward sharply, and the water becomes much deeper. In most places the ocean floor is between 10,000 and 20,000 feet below the water's surface. That's about 3,000 to 6,000 meters. But there is one spot in the Pacific Ocean that's 36,198 feet, or 10,860 meters, deep. That's nearly 7 miles! This spot is Challenger Deep in the Marianas Trench, and it's the deepest part of the ocean.

There are also underwater mountains. Some belong to mountain ranges. One of the longest mountain ranges is the Mid-Atlantic Ridge. It's in the middle of the Atlantic Ocean.

When is a mountain an island?

Some underwater mountains are so high they rise up out of the water and form islands. Bermuda, the Hawaiian Islands, and the Azores, a group of islands west of Portugal, are really the tops of huge underwater mountains.

In the Arctic and Antarctic Oceans, there is another kind of "mountain." It's a floating mountain of ice called an iceberg. Icebergs are a danger to ships. That's because only a small part of an iceberg can be seen. A captain may think the ship is far away from an iceberg. But suddenly there is a scraping, crunching sound. The ship has struck the hidden part of the ice mountain—the part that is underwater.

27

In 1912, there was a huge ocean liner that people thought was unsinkable. But it hit an iceberg. A hole was torn in the ship's side, and it sank. The ship was the *Titanic*. Today, an International Ice Patrol watches for floating icebergs. When the Patrol finds one, they warn the captains of ships to stay away from the danger area.

Sometimes sailors are glad to see an iceberg.

That's because icebergs are made of frozen fresh water, not salty ocean water. Sailors can't drink ocean water—but if they cut off a piece of an iceberg, they can drink fresh water as the ice melts.

People who study the ocean are called *oceanographers.* Some of the first oceanographers studied the currents. What they learned helped to make ocean travel safer. Today, oceanographers are studying how plants and animals live in the ocean. What they learn may help us get more food and other resources from the ocean.

Oceanographers are also studying the ocean floor. That's not always easy. When oceanographers go down into the ocean, the weight of the water presses on them. As they go deeper, the pressure grows greater. If they go too deep, the pressure can crush them. So special submarines were designed to safely take oceanographers deep under the water. With these special submarines, oceanographers can study the deepest parts of the ocean. But the ocean floor is so vast that only a very small part of it has been studied.

Can the ocean solve our problems?

Many people believe the ocean can help solve some of the world's greatest problems. Today, scientists are looking to the ocean for energy, for minerals, and for food. For the ocean is much more than a huge body of water. It is a vast storehouse of natural resources.

A fascinating world lies beneath the ocean's surface—a special world waiting to be discovered.